A Vestry Member's Guide

revised edition

A Vestry Member's Guide

Van S. Bowen

A Vestry Member's Guide
was sponsored by
The Episcopal Church Foundation

HarperSanFrancisco
A Division of HarperCollins*Publishers*

Library of Congress Catalog Card Number: 76–44386
ISBN: 0–86683–872–9

91   92   93   94   95   SEM   17   16   15   14   13   12   11   10

Foreword

In recent years lay men and women have begun to exercise more of their rightful share of the ministry of our Church, a trend that will gather momentum in the foreseeable future. An important part of this ministry is service on the parish vestry, whose members represent their congregations in the parish's relations with its clergy and in the management of its corporate property.

As the management team of the parish, the vestry is responsible not only for an accountability to the congregation, but also for providing strong, creative leadership as it works with the clergy to set the tone and direction of parish life.

Open, frank communication among parishioners, vestry and rector will promote mutual confidence and point the way toward the positive action so vital to the well-being of a strong parish.

The diversity of our Church's membership and the variety of congregational styles gives us many strengths from which to draw purpose and resolve. Different vestries reflect these strengths in different ways, and no two go about their work in exactly the same fashion. But certain problems are common to all.

This guide describes the structures that may be adapted by vestries to suit their own personalities and traditions and makes suggestions for promoting the healthy parish life on which our Church is grounded.

I believe you will find it helpful and am happy to commend it to you.

JOHN M. ALLIN
Presiding Bishop of The Episcopal Church

Acknowledgments

In revising this text, I am grateful to the Rev. Roddey Reid, Jr., for his advice on the process of calling a new rector. The Rev. Dr. Thomas A. Carson and Richard M. Lamport have shed light on the growing importance of planned giving and Mrs. Margaret Andersen on the organization of the national Church's Executive Council.

Some years ago, when this guide was first written, three clergymen in the Diocese of Washington pressed for a clear emphasis on the contemporary in its development. I am still indebted to the Rev. James B. Anderson, the Rev. John C. Harris and the Rev. Loren B. Mead for their incisive criticism and exciting vision of what a parish can be.

The Rev. John A. Schultz has kindly provided statistical information, and Frederick L. Redpath has been especially helpful in bringing certain phases of parish life up to date.

I am obligated to each of these and to the many others whose steady encouragement is warmly appreciated.

V. S. B.

Contents

Preface

The vestry as we know it today is a distinctly American institution in the local government of the Church.

It was not until the late Middle Ages that a layman was given official recognition in the parish as churchwarden, with the responsibility for keeping the nave of the church in good repair. Until that time the clergy had been in undisputed control of parish property and whatever income it might produce, as well as the conduct of all religious services.

This opening wedge into the solid wall of ecclesiastical prerogative was gradually extended until, by the time of the Tudors in England, the whole parish met as a vestry, with any resident eligible to attend. These meetings were held in the room where the vestments were kept and took its name—the vestry.

When the first settlements were taking root along the Atlantic seaboard of this country in the seventeenth century, many congregations in the Church of England had entrusted certain parish functions to the hands of a "select vestry," numbering between twelve and twenty-four men, who elected their wardens, collected church taxes, and took charge of parish property. English immigrants brought this rudimentary form of church government with them to the Colony of Virginia, and it was subsequently established, with local variations, in other colonies up and down the coast.

During the next 150 years, until the American Revolution snapped the reins of authority tenaciously held by the English

Church and Crown, the "select vestry" was shaped and refined by often fiery controversy between Church and State, on the one hand, and the colonists on the other. Issues that we take for granted today were bitterly contested. Who had the right to appoint a parish clergyman—the vestry or the royal governor? Were vestries to be elected by the parish or appointed by the rector? What was the limit of their responsibilities? When the War of Independence was brought to a successful conclusion, most of these matters were resolved in favor of the vestries, although it was not until 1904 that a General Convention of our Church wrote into national Church law a formal definition of the vestry and its duties.

Entitled "Of Parish Vestries," Canon 13 of Title I is brief and to the point:

Sec. 1. In every Parish of this Church the number, mode of selection, and term of office of Wardens and members of the Vestry, with the qualifications of voters, shall be such as the State or Diocesan law may permit or require, and the Wardens and members of the Vestry selected under such law shall hold office until their successors are selected and have qualified.

Sec. 2. Except as provided by the law of the State or of the Diocese, the Vestry shall be agents and legal representatives of the Parish in all matters concerning its corporate property and the relations of the Parish to its Clergy.

Sec. 3. Unless it conflicts with the law as aforesaid, the Rector, when present, shall preside in all the meetings of the Vestry.

It should be noted that national canon law is written by the Church's General Convention, which meets every three years, and applies throughout the Church. Diocesan canon law must be approved by the diocesan convention and governs local usage, much as the laws of the fifty states supplement federal legislation.

The right to vote in federal elections that was recently won by eighteen-year-olds has been reflected in many dioceses by a comparable change in canon law so that young people may now vote for their vestry members and even stand for election themselves.

Unless state law directs to the contrary, a vestry is composed of "Rector, Wardens, and Vestry members." The number of vestry members is to some extent a matter of parish preference within the context of diocesan canon law, which prescribes the minimum and maximum size.

The churchwarden, as noted above, first made his appearance in the parish structure of the Middle Ages. Each vestry in the Episcopal Church today has two, customarily known as senior and junior wardens. National canon law makes the wardens jointly responsible, with the minister and vestry, for providing information to the bishop on "the state of the Congregation" when he visits a parish (Title III, Canon 21, Sec. 2-d).

The wardens must notify the bishop when their rector retires or resigns or the parish falls vacant for any other reason, and send written notice to the bishop when a new rector has been elected (III, 23, Sec. 1 and 3). The canons describe how, if a minister neglects to perform regular services for his congregation, from disability or any other cause, and refuses to permit another priest to officiate, the wardens or vestry, with the bishop's written consent, "have power . . . to permit any duly qualified Minister of this Church to officiate." (III, 21, Sec. 5-b).

The canons also stipulate that, in the rector's absence or vacancy, the wardens or vestry shall not "permit any person to officiate . . . without sufficient evidence of his being duly licensed or ordained to minister in this Church." (III, 25).

Such is the bare framework put together over the centuries by custom, practice, and canon law. It provides great flexibility to the vestry in organizing itself and permits a variety of approaches to the structure of the parish. These choices will be developed in some detail on the pages that follow.

It is often easy, while concentrating on vestry members' duties and responsibilities, to lose sight of their spiritual calling to greater things. This is a task which every vestry member will also want to pursue to the best of his or her ability.

In September, 1976, the General Convention voted to change canon law to provide for the ordination of women to the priesthood and episcopate, having authorized their ordination as deacons three years earlier at the previous General Convention. In the pages that follow, the terms rector, vicar, curate, assistant, or bishop apply to both ordained men and women of the Church. The masculine pronoun is occasionally used generically to refer to both.

I

Your Parish
or Mission

After keeping sedate step with the times for much of its
history, the parish has recently come face-to-face with an explo-
sive chain of developments for which it was little prepared by
tradition or experience.

During the 1950s, and at an accelerating pace in the sixties
and seventies, our population has become more mobile and
rootless. Communities in both city and countryside have changed
and with them the expectations of those who live there. The
rallying cry of equal rights for women has won widespread
acceptance, and, as an aftermath of a flourishing youth culture,
young people now assert their independence with vigorous de-
fense of their opinions. The voice of authority seldom goes
unchallenged, while the structures on which society has rested
securely are called into serious question. Buffeted by winds of
change, many of our institutions have sought to adapt themselves to the demands of suddenly vocal constituencies.

While intensified problems cry out for immediate solution,
your parish cannot stand idly by. It must respond creatively to
the human and community needs that force themselvs upon
your congregations through the lives of your parishioners.

Webster's Dictionary defines a parish as "the ecclesiastical
unit of [an] area comitted to one pastor" and also as "the resi-

dents of such [an] area. . . ." A mission may be similarly defined, except that it is not an independent entity like the parish.

While canon law concerning missions varies from one diocese to another, certain elements are common to all. Unlike a parish, a mission is not incorporated and derives a substantial portion of its support from the diocese or a nearby parish; title to its real property is vested in the diocese. The priest in charge is the vicar, appointed by the bishop to serve at his pleasure and to act under his direction or that of the appropriate diocesan department. In some dioceses, the bishop also appoints one or two wardens and a mission treasurer.

Known variously as the Bishop's Committee, the Mission Council or the mission's Executive Committee, the mission's equivalent of the parish vestry concerns itself with the temporal affairs of the congregation, principally with property maintenance and finances. Its members are also appointed by the bishop, if canon law so provides, or they are elected by the congregation for fixed terms of office. The vicar acts as chairman at regular meetings of this Council or Committee, and their mutual goal is to move toward independent, self-supporting and self-governing parish status.

The dual nature of the parish or mission is apparent at once from Webster's definition: a self-contained congregation under the care of a priest, as well as individual men, women, and children living nearby. As a social unit, the parish is subject to much of the stress that is taxing the resiliency of our universities, courts, and government at every level of administration. On a personal level, the men, women, and young people who live within the parish bounds have their own hopes and needs to be satisfied through the congregational life of the parish.

Everyone works out—and lives—his own statement of what it means to be a Christian. The Westminster Shorter Catechism says that "man's chief end is to glorify God and enjoy Him forever," and while this ringing declaration is rarely uppermost in our minds as we go about earning a living or bringing up our children, it surely echoes in our thoughts. The response of a group, the congregation, to the question of how to glorify God promises a greater, and conceivably an entirely different, potential than the sum of individual replies. But first the group must be heard, and not every congregation is in the habit of speaking its mind.

How can you as a vestry member come to grips with the complex problems created by differences in age groups and life styles, attitudes toward worship and authority that are so distinct today? Once you become better known as a member of the vestry, people will turn to you with their complaints and criticism, which is normal and natural. But a great deal more is called for than mere willingness to listen. Communication is the key to action, and it follows naturally that the manner in which vestry members respond to the diversity in their parish is crucial for its vitality.

A sound first step to opening communication between you and the parishioners you represent is to look searchingly at your parish together. In what ways has your congregation changed in the past ten years? Has attendance leveled off or dropped sharply? Is your church school in trouble? How can you help newcomers to the parish move rapidly into full, active membership? Are there better ways than the gathering of statistics to determine how an imaginative parish program can best serve your community? The parishioners' answers to these and other significant questions will contribute to a sense of direction that can be vital to your parish's future.

In some parishes the vestry and the rector identify specific needs in specific areas and carry the resulting parish profile to the congregation, both individually and at town hall meetings, so that the parishioners themselves may help to refine the profile and participate in transforming strategy into action. Other parishes initiate the process in discussion groups when members examine what they want their parish to accomplish and how to bring this about.

The ultimate aim of communication between you and the congregation, between you and the rector, and between parishioners themselves is to stimulate a continuing interchange that leads to a clear understanding of purpose at any given time. Your role in this ongoing, dynamic procedure demands tact and skill, to keep constantly in touch with the congregation's disparate views as they shift and turn to new directions. Your responsibility is to weave these often conflicting views into the growing fabric of parish life.

Once a congregation has moved from isolated pockets of silence into open, easy communication, it escapes from being locked into rigid structure to an exciting arena of fresh confidence and self-assurance. It will have grown much closer to the original definition of the parish, which is derived from two Greek words that mean "away from home." The early Christians saw themselves as wanderers, joined together in an earthly pilgrimage to their heavenly home. Their belief can speak to us today, if we will listen.

II

Your Rector

Canon law, as we have seen, makes the vestry the parish's legal representatives in relations with its clergy and states that the rector shall preside at all vestry meetings when he or she is present. But what is said about the rector?

Title III, Canon 21 vests him with "control of the worship and the spiritual jurisdiction of the Parish" and places under his authority "all assistant Ministers of the Parish, by whatever name they may be designated." It says he is entitled to the use of parish buildings and their equipment at all times "for the purposes of his office and for the full and free discharge of all functions and duties pertaining thereto."

The canon goes on to stipulate that the undesignated offerings received at Holy Communion on one Sunday each month shall be deposited in the rector's discretionary fund and, in conclusion, makes the rector responsible for maintaining the parish register, which records "all Baptisms, Confirmations, Marriages, Burials, and the names of all Communicants."

These, then, are the boundaries set by church law within which the complex relationship between vestry and rector grows, takes shape, and, it is to be hoped, flourishes. The canons' explicit division of parish life into the spiritual and the temporal, assigned to the rector and to the vestry, can be misleading, however, in its oversimplification.

A parish is people, and no rector, no matter how gifted of tongue or devout in piety, can minister to the spiritual needs of a congregation in a vacuum. He or she needs the confidence and constant support of the vestry to strengthen programs already under way and to introduce possible new modes or means of worship or mission. This is vital, for the vestry's control of the purse strings gives it the power to restrict or to throttle any parish activity of which it disapproves.

Conversely, the vestry is made accountable by canon law for the management of all parish property, but it would be foolish to assume that this trust could be carried out without the close collaboration of the rector. He or she spends a large part of every day on the premises and is the first to know when the roof leaks or the furnace breaks down. Seeing that the buildings are kept in good repair and bills are paid promptly are final responsibilities of the vestry, to be sure, but the rector often handles these matters on the spot.

Mutual trust and candor between you and your rector are essential for building the sort of cooperative teamwork that provides decisive parish leadership. But there are stumbling blocks. It is quite possible that you and the rector have different opinions on the vestry's function in parish administration or, for that matter, on the roles each should play. You may disagree about various parish programs and the relative emphasis assigned to each. What you expect from the Church may be far removed from what your rector is seeking and attempting to give. The most difficult part of all may be overcoming your inhibitions against expressing your disagreement.

Differences like these can also divide a vestry and seriously affect or impede its decision-making process. Unless you and your rector deliberately provide for periods of frank discussion and debate, the way is open to critical conflict. By cultivating the ability to disagree with each other openly and dispassionately, you make it much less likely that other members of the vestry will seek to avoid tension by remaining silent.

A basic issue of power underlies the relationship between your clergy and your congregation. The extent to which your rector or vicar shares authority and the challenges he offers to you as a vestry member and to other parishioners can create a positive tension to stimulate growth in the life of your parish or mission. By the same token, the pressures exerted by the laity are necessary ingredients for the steady development of clergy skills and performance. This "we-they" syndrome is an inescapable part of your service on the vestry; when welcomed and affirmed as a means of growth, it can work to the advantage of everyone involved.

In many dioceses vestries are urged to enter into written agreements with their clergy, especially when a new rector is called. These letters of agreement, which must be in accordance with the provisions of canon law, outline for the rector his or her duties and compensation, the use of church buildings, and the staff services to be furnished. They usually provide for an annual review as well, which is particularly pertinent in these days of rapid change. You should realize that what you expect from your rector may vary markedly from what your colleagues look for, which will probably not coincide exactly with your rector's own concept. It is up to you to see that differences are aired in a straightforward fashion, by businesslike procedures like the annual review. If this evaluation takes the form of a mutual appraisal of the past year, with rector and vestry together scanning the parish's successes and disappointments, it can be especially revealing, confronting problems that have developed on either side before they become entrenched into immutable positions.

A word about the role of your curate or assistant minister would be appropriate here. Vestries find that a written job description indicating his or her rights and duties as specifically as possible, as well as his compensation and formal relationship to the rector and to the vestry itself, creates a more benign climate than when no such document exists. The relationship between curate and rector can only too often become clouded by misunderstanding, dissatisfaction, even distrust. The sensitive vestry is aware of these dangers and, without impinging on the rector's prerogatives, does all it can to prevent them.

Your vestry may recognize the wisdom of writing into the letter of agreement with your rector a paragraph that urges him to continue his professional development. It is common practice these days for business and industrial executives to attend refresher courses or training seminars to keep abreast of innovations in their field so that they may make full use of their abilities. In an area demanding as many skills as contemporary parish leadership, the need of the clergy for continuing education should not have to be justified. You can help your rector design his plans to take into account the special needs of your church, so that the time and money invested in his studies will be of immediate benefit to the parish.

An increasing number of clergy are turning to their vestries for help with liturgical development. Because changes in the forms of worship are a threat to the composure of many congregations and can often lead to outraged feelings, vestry members are sometimes asked to serve on a liturgical committee and draw up plans for the introduction of new services. Arranging discussions about the liturgy well in advance of any change, and a well-publicized schedule that offers the familiar service as an alternative, will go far to remove initial hostility. Your congregation's response will of course be a determining factor in deciding your future course.

This is not to imply that you, as a member of the vestry, should attempt to dictate which liturgy is to be used on Sunday morning, any more than the rector should force on you his priority targets for the annual parish budget. Such a state of affairs may have occurred two or three hundred years ago in colonial America and, it must be admitted, still crops up now and then. How much better it is to offer suggestions to your rector—and to listen to your constituents so that your proposals reflect a broader opinion. You may be surprised at how enthusiastically your comments are welcomed. And how much better to seek your rector's advice, which is not the same as following it blindly, on the many occasions when training and experience have given him insight and expertise.

By virtue of his or her position, the rector knows personally more of the congregation than anyone else in the parish and can often suggest an expert when the vestry is looking for someone to help with insurance or rewiring an electric system. Despite the vestry's status in law as agents of the parish, it is the rector—who is also a member of the vestry—who provides a living bridge between the two, who knows the interests of the parishioners and can call on them when needed.

You and your rector, each in your own way, share a common purpose and collegial interest: to help the parish open itself to the meaning of life, the life of every man, woman, and child, as revealed to us all by Jesus Christ. This is no easy task and will sometimes seem beyond the reach of any human. But when confidence, understanding, and good will have forged a true partnership between vestry and rector, the goal is already in view.

III

Your Bishop

After the Roman Emperor Constantine made Christianity a lawful religion throughout the empire in 313, the struggling Church of the first centuries after Christ was rapidly transformed into a tightly knit structure based on the efficient model of imperial government. It would be no exaggeration to say that the contemporary bishop was a key person in this transformation, the local equivalent in church administration of his counterpart in the state, the regional governor. He was known in Latin as "episcopus," a term our Episcopal Church has chosen for its name, so that we are known, literally, as a Church that has bishops.

As the Church was torn by doctrinal strife and schism, culminating in the Protestant Reformation, the episcopal form of administration was firmly maintained by the Roman Catholic, the Orthodox, and our own Anglican communion in an unbroken line of succession. In cutting themselves loose from this tradition, other Churches not only reformed dogma, but introduced entirely new forms of church government such as the congregationalist, in which the local congregation became, in effect, an independent entity.

An Episcopal bishop performs a variety of functions, each vital to the life and growth of the Church of which your parish is a living part. He preserves the Church's continuity by confirming new members, ordaining priests and deacons, and assisting in consecrating bishops. He is the chief administrator of a diocese, the regional grouping of parishes and missions that fall under his jurisdiction. He must approve the candidacies of young men and women from these congregations who want to study for the ministry at theological seminary, and the diocesan Standing Committee must pass on their qualifications, after initial screening by the Commission on Ministry, before they can be ordained at his hands. He is chief pastor and counselor to all clergy in the diocese and, when differences arise between a rector and a congregation or vestry, may be asked to mediate the dispute. From time to time he may arrange training conferences or orientation sessions for the wardens in the diocese. He is automatically a member of the House of Bishops which, with the elected House of Deputies, forms the legislative arm of our Church, its General Convention.

In larger dioceses, such a work load would outstrip the abilities of any person, so that the diocesan bishop is often assisted by one or two other bishops, elected by diocesan convention. A suffragan is an assistant with no right of succession, while a coadjutor is elected to succeed the diocesan bishop when he retires or dies in office, taking some of the load from his shoulders in the meantime. In recent years it has become increasingly common practice for a bishop who has already been consecrated to be called by a diocesan bishop to work with him, with the consent of the Standing Committee and the approval of the diocesan convention. He is known as an assistant bishop and serves at the discretion of the diocesan bishop.

Just as your rector turns to you and your vestry colleagues for help in running the parish, your bishop is assisted by a comparable group of lay persons and clergy known as the executive council of the diocese. Some of its members are elected, either by the annual diocesan convention or by local assemblies of parishes and missions, and some are appointed by the bishop to carry out the convention's program for the diocese in the ensuing year. Diocesan councils are organized in several ways: some are divided into program departments, such as Stewardship, Mission, or perhaps Urban Affairs or Youth, while others are set up as task forces that are regrouped from time to time, according to changing needs.

In 1973 the General Convention wrote into national canon law a provision that a Commission on Ministry, composed of clergy and lay persons, should be organized in every diocese to "assist the Bishop in determining present and future needs for Ministry in the Diocese, and in matters pertaining to the enlist-ment and selection of persons for Ministry" (Title III, Canon 1, Sec. 3). The Commission was further charged with responsibility for interviewing each candidate before his or her ordination to the diaconate; for "the guidance and pastoral care of Deacons," and with assisting "the Bishop in matters pertaining to the continuing education" of the clergy. In many dioceses, it is this Commission which is now developing programs for Christian education and lay ministry, both matters of not inconsiderable interest to you as a vestry member. Representatives of this Commission usually sit on the diocesan council as well.

Your bishop's staff includes a number of professionals who, to do their work well, must be familiar with what parishes in your diocese—and in other dioceses—are doing in their fields of competence, so that they become excellent sources of infor-mation and advice. When your parish encounters difficulties, a specialist from the diocese can often tell you how other parishes have dealt with similar circumstances, why some have succeed-ed when others failed. But your vestry and rector have first to ask for aid, which presupposes an acquaintance with the organi-zation of the diocese and the sort of assistance it is equipped to give.

When you attend your first vestry meeting and listen to the treasurer's report, you will notice that your parish pays a certain sum to the diocese each year, which is fixed according to a standard schedule. A part of this pays the housekeeping ex-penses of the diocese, and another portion is transmitted to the national Church. What remains is devoted to the mission work of the diocese. In a practical sense, this work is a joint, cooperative venture in which your parish and all other parishes in the diocese join to support a slate of projects that no single congregation could underwrite by itself.

Perhaps most significant on the list are mission churches in the inner city or in rural areas, where the congregation cannot yet pay its way and relies on help from the diocese to keep its doors open. You may be a member of the Bishop's Committee for a mission church and know first-hand that, without this help, you could not pay your vicar's salary or for the upkeep of your church building.

Some dioceses work with Indians and maintain special programs for young people or the aging. Others support campus ministries, services to the deaf and blind, prison chaplaincies, or inner-city missions. Each demands a high degree of professional expertise which your parish helps to provide through its annual transfer of funds.

How can you as a member of the vestry influence and, to some degree, channel your diocese's efforts in directions you believe they should take? A first answer, clearly, is to become familiar with the organization of your bishop's office and to meet the men and women who work there. They will be eager to discuss what they are doing, since a well-informed constituency among the parishes works to the advantage of the entire diocese. As you learn more of the rationale behind a particular piece of program, your suggestions for a change of emphasis or an entirely new departure can be put more cogently where they will have the most effect.

A second, more direct means of influencing diocesan policy is the annual convention of the diocese. Your diocesan canon law specifies how many members of the laity are to be chosen as convention delegates from each parish and mission and what proportion, if any, should be from the vestry. All clergy resident in the diocese are eligible to attend and vote. Besides filling diocesan offices by election—and electing a new bishop when his chair becomes vacant—the convention lays down policies for the bishop's staff and executive council to follow in the year ahead. Choosing delegates to represent your parish at the convention demands the same careful attention that you give to studying the agenda in advance, so that your representatives will have a chance to determine where the parish stands on items to be discussed. After the convention, ask your rector and your lay delegates how money is being spent in your diocese and for what purposes.

These days a growing number of bishops are spending more time with each parish in the diocese, even if it means less frequent visits than before. When your bishop comes, you have a ready-made opportunity to ask hard questions about the directions the diocese is following or the policies of the national Church. In reply to a candid expression of your views, he will tend to be equally frank, so that you open the door to greater mutual comprehension, which is just as necessary for him as for you.

In our episcopal structure, the bishop stands at the heart of the diocese. Through his hands the Church is perpetually renewed and, in his actions, finds new meaning for its mission of service to all of humanity.

IV

Duties of the Vestry

No uniform approach to the orientation of new vestry members has yet been devised, although several prominent landmarks guide the way. Your rector or senior warden will very likely give you copies of the parish bylaws and diocesan canon law, as well as the minutes of recent meetings to bring you up to date on current issues you will soon have to deal with. A copy of the *Constitution and Canons of The Episcopal Church* would also be helpful.

The thoughtful neophyte, however, will want to ask questions, both to learn more about the parish and to take the measure of his new colleagues so that he and they may begin to work together from the start with a maximum of shared information and trust. Newcomers to the vestry should be encouraged to ask for clarification and feel entitled to full explanations. A vestry, for instance, has two distinct modes of operation, which may not be clear at first: it functions as a legislative and administrative board according to parliamentary procedure; but it also engages in program development in a much less structured fashion, which entails an entirely different approach to the way it works.

To clarify relationships and create the common understanding needed to function smoothly as a team, some vestries spend a weekend getting to know each other after every election of new members. Planned sessions like these can offer excellent orientation, with the valuable by-product of identifying new members' talents and skills that can be put to good use in the parish.

The agenda for a vestry retreat can also list the re-examination of parish goals, as well as a revision of the parish self-study or profile, which it is wise to keep up to date. Vestries that employ an outside consultant to help plan and conduct these sessions discover, as a rule, that their discussions are more sharply focused and illuminating.

Your own imagination and creativity have a definite part in the vestry's deliberations. Too often it falls to your rector to suggest innovations in program or direction, while the vestry reacts with cautious prudence. How much healthier will it be when you and your colleagues propose that the parish embark on pioneering experiments to satisfy some of the needs you encounter every day in your lives and work? Turning a careful ear to the men and women in the congregation whose professional backgrounds expose them to fresh ideas will also help you to make the vestry an active partner with your rector in setting the parish on a progressive course.

Two matters sometimes overlooked deserve special mention here. One has to do with the pastoral responsibility of the vestry, particularly the senior warden, for your clergy. Your rector needs a friend to whom he can turn in moments of doubt, exasperation, and elation, too. He needs one who will listen to personal problems and urge him to relax when he works too hard, who will plan with him a joint response to any looming controversy, who will be a confidant to his family as well. Each member of the vestry can help with this.

The second matter, which occurs infrequently, concerns your vestry's reaction when asked to recommend to your bishop someone from the parish who wants to be ordained. Canon law requires that you and your rector act in effect as sponsors, a procedure designed to weed out undesirable candidates. In the past, approval has often been granted automatically with little regard for the individual's ability or suitability for the ordained ministry. If the high calibre of the Church's clergy is to be sustained, however, your vestry should look carefully into the applicant's qualifications before deciding whether or not to recommend him or her. Canon law specifies the form in which your recommendation must be submitted (III, 2, Sec. 4) and that your recommendation must be reaffirmed as your candidate moves through the process (III, 3, Sec. 2-c).

We have already noted that the chief officers of every vestry are its junior warden and senior warden, sometimes known as the people's warden and the rector's warden, respectively, because in certain dioceses the senior warden is named by the rector rather than elected at the annual parish meeting. The vestry often chooses one of its members as clerk, to keep minutes of vestry meetings, and another as treasurer, although neither officer need be a member of the vestry and can be named from among qualified parishioners. The bylaws of most parishes also provide that an executive committee, consisting of the rector, the wardens, and one or two vestry members, shall be empowered to act on matters demanding attention between meetings of the full vestry.

The management of parish property and its financial resources, for which the vestry is ultimately responsible, is frequently divided among several people or groups in a manner to be described in the next chapter. As agent of the vestry, it is the treasurer's duty to submit the parish budget for the approval of the vestry every year and to make a financial report at each of its monthly meetings. Two forms in common use for this purpose are reproduced on the following pages and can be adapted for your own uses. They summarize receipts and disbursements for the month in question and list cumulative totals for the year to date, which are then compared to the budgeted figures for the same period. These forms, or suitable variations,

PARISH TREASURER'S MONTHLY REPORT TO VESTRY
(prepared on the cash basis)

_____ Parish at _____ Month of_____, 19___

Dated_____Signed _____ Treasurer

	RECEIPTS	Month	Year to Date	Budget
	For Parish Support:			
1.	Plate collections......................................	$.............	$.............	$.............
2.	Pledges and subscriptions...............................	....	....	....
3.	Church school................................	....	....	....
4.	Parish organizations.............................	....	....	....
5.	Other sources	....	....	....
a.	....	....	....	....
b.	....	....	....	....
c.	....	....	....	....
d.	....	....	....	....
e.	....	....	....	....
6.	Investment income............................	....	....	....
	For Designated Parochial Purposes:			
7.	Communion alms............................	....	....	....
8.	Designated gifts for the Parish........................	....	....	....
9.	Investment income............................ ..	....	....	....
	For Work Outside Parish:			
10.	Missionary and general church program.........	....	....	....
11.	Special offerings	....	....	....
	Legacies and Other Donations (non-recurring)			
12.	Legacies and bequests............................	....	....	....
13.	Other donations to capital	....	....	....
14.	Capital gains (or losses).....	....	....	....
15.	Sale of Investments or Property (incl. savings accounts)........................	....	....	....
16.	Money Borrowed.......................................	....	....	....
17.	Exchanges...................................	....	....	....
	TOTAL RECEIPTS:	$_____	$_____	$_____

SUMMARY

	Month	Year to Date	Budget
Total Receipts (per above).....................................	$.............	$.............	$.............
Total Disbursements (per page 2)........................	_____	_____	_____
Excess (Deficit) of Receipts over Disbursements..	$.............	$.............	$.............
Add Beginning Bank Balance................................	_____	_____	_____
Bank Balance—End of Period (see below)...........	$_____	$_____	$_____

ALLOCATION OF CASH FUNDS

Checking account—allocated to Special Funds.... $.............
     —available for general parish
     purposes .... _____
     Total (per above)................... $.............
Savings accounts—allocated to Special Funds..... ....
     —available for general parish
     purposes................................ _____

        $_____

PARISH TREASURER'S MONTHLY REPORT TO VESTRY

DISBURSEMENTS

For Current Expenses—Parish:	Month	Year to Date	Budget
18. Salaries:			
a. Rector's salary	$	$	$ ....
b.	....	....	....
c.	....	....	....
d.	....	....	....
e.	....	....	....
f.	....	....	....
19. Social security taxes	....	....	....
20. Insurance premiums	....	....	....
21. Fuel, light, water and power	....	....	....
22a. Office supplies and postage	....	....	....
22b. Church school supplies	....	....	....
23. Auto and travel expense	....	....	....
24. Telephone and telegraph	....	....	....
25. Altar supplies	....	....	....
26. Music, choir supplies and maintenance	....	....	....
27. Bookkeeping and auditing	....	....	....
28. Other parish expense	....	....	....
....	....	....	....
....	....	....	....
....	....	....	....
TOTAL CURRENT EXPENSE	$ _____	$ _____	$ _____
29. Pension Premiums	....	....	....
30. Diocesan Assessments	....	....	....
For Special Parochial Purposes:			
31. Communion Alms	....	....	....
32. Rental property expense	....	....	....
33.	....	....	....
34. Chapel or parochial mission expense	....	....	....
35. Repairs and minor improvements	....	....	....
36. Interest paid	....	....	....
37. Taxes	....	....	....
38. Rent	....	....	....
39. Other special parochial purposes	....	....	....
Diocesan and General Church Missionary Program:	....	....	....
40. Missionary Fund assessments	....	....	....
41. Special offerings	....	....	....
42. Major Improvements and Additions to Property	....	....	....
43. Purchase of Investments (incl. Savings Accts.)	....	....	....
44. Payments on Loans—principal	....	....	....
45. Exchanges	....	....	....
....	....	....	....
TOTAL DISBURSEMENTS	$ _____	$ _____	$ _____

enable you to detect at a glance such trouble spots as heavy, unexpected expenses or flagging income, so that action may be taken to prevent the situation from becoming critical later in the year.

A strong case can often be made for routing the payment of all bills and the crediting of all income through the parish treasurer or an authorized assistant, for this is good business practice and sound accounting procedure. It may be that your women's or young people's group has for a long time staged its own fund-raising events and bazaars, for which it has settled the accounts, and from which it often contributes the proceeds to the parish budget. Each case must, of course, stand on its own merits—and there are sometimes compelling reasons for not introducing a centralized payment system—but the fact that more and more parishes are changing to a unified system of handling their accounts speaks for itself.

The requirements of canon law in regard to managing parish property are scrupulously spelled out in Title I, Canon 6, "Of Business Methods in Church Affairs," which you will want to know well. All trust and permanent funds as well as securities are to be deposited with federal or state banks or with agencies approved in writing by the diocesan Finance Committee. Detailed records are to be kept for these funds, and treasurers or custodians are to be bonded. Account books must be maintained and audited annually, with a certificate of the audit of your parish's financial reports for the previous twelve months to be sent to your bishop no later than September 1 each year. All buildings and their contents are to be adequately insured, and the Finance Committee of your diocese may require that copies of any or all of these accounts be filed with it. The fiscal year is to begin January 1. The canon also states that no "real property for any Parish, Mission, Congregation, or Institution" can be mortgaged without the written consent of your bishop and Standing Committee unless diocesan canon law prescribes otherwise, and that all such property is held in trust for the

Episcopal Church. Title I, Canon 6 is printed in full on the last pages of this Guide.

The Executive Council of the national Church has printed "A Manual of Accounting Principles and Reporting Practices for Episcopal Dioceses, Parishes, and Missions" to "establish uniform accounting and financial reporting systems that will serve the Episcopal Church and carry out the changes contained in Canon 6." The manual may be ordered from The Seabury Press, 815 Second Avenue, New York, N.Y. 10017.

The Finance Department of the Executive Council has also published a loose-leaf Parish Cash Book, together with an instruction manual, as a guide for parish treasurers not trained in accounting. This is also available from The Seabury Press and contains instructions, with sample forms, for recording your parish's:

> disbursements
> receipts
> handling of special funds
> securities
> bank transfers
> statistical information for diocesan use
> withholding of income tax

National canon law (II, 7) makes it unlawful for a vestry "to encumber or alienate any dedicated or consecrated Church or Chapel . . . without the previous consent of the Bishop." It adds that no church or chapel "shall be removed, taken down, or otherwise disposed of for any worldly or common use, without the previous consent of the Standing Committee of the Diocese."

The bylaws of your parish probably set a given day each month for vestry meetings, such as the third Tuesday, which permits you to plan ahead and be sure to attend. Since your parish qualifies as a corporation under the laws of your state, you will want to pay attention to what the laws say about a quorum at vestry meetings. The timing of your meetings is also important, for if they are held over lunch as in some parishes, mothers with small children or some working men and women might never be able to attend and would thus be effectively barred from membership.

The agenda for your meetings is important in determining how you approach questions of basic interest to the whole parish. How are critical matters assured of frank discussion by the vestry? How do you make sure that human considerations are not forgotten in your concentration on property mainte-nance or fiscal matters? Some vestries respond by inviting every member to add items of his or her own at a certain stage of the meeting. The constant threat of isolation from the views and expectations of the parishioners they represent has led a num-ber of vestries to appoint one of their members as ombudsman for communications, to work for a continuing, open interchange of ideas between vestry and congregation. You may find the professional advice of a process consultant helpful with this and with using the information you receive to redefine your pro-gram objectives.

How do you handle criticism of your clergy? When you dis-agree with what your rector is doing or what he or she proposes to do, how do you oppose constructively? There is, obviously, no pat reply. But an awareness of the complicated nature of human relationships can illuminate some of the problems thrust upon you by election to the vestry. The annual review described above, in which you and the rector explore your differing con-cepts of roles and programs, is another step toward problem solving. Differences do occur, and they always will. But their inevitable impact can be softened and sometimes turned to positive advantage by conscious efforts to bring them into the open, where they can be recognized, probed and talked about together.

V

Parish Structure

The structure of your parish today is the creature of many yesterdays, which have given shape and substance to its present form. But no living organism can remain unchanged, frozen in time. The financial and administrative relationships that have grown up between vestry and parish organizations like the Laymen's League or the Women of the Church, for example, need to be re-examined from time to time for the better understanding of both. Some parishes have moved far beyond mere re-examination of internal relationships to the point of arranging to share space with congregations of different faiths, while a few others have decided never to own any real estate.

Like any undertaking that involves all sorts and conditions of men and women, a parish is stamped with the imprint of strong personalities. It must struggle with an inertia that says, "We have always done it this way." If you are not to abdicate your responsibilities, you and your fellow vestry members must constantly strive, in careful collaboration with your rector, for a harmonious balance between the old and the new, between the safe, comfortable customs of the past and the untried, challenging innovations of the future.

It should be emphasized from the start that there is no ideal organizational pattern for a vestry to choose. What succeeds brilliantly in one parish can fall apart dismally in another. The right structure for you is the one that works best in your own circumstances. But as the personality of your parish changes, your plan of organization needs to grow with it to reflect new conditions and new aspirations among your parishioners. Structure is of secondary importance to the ways in which you are able to identify and satisfy the spiritual and social needs and desires of the congregation you serve.

Before describing four types of parish organization from which vestries pick and choose elements for their own use, it is worth considering what makes any of them tick. A paramount question is one of accountability: Who initiates action? Who follows through to completion? Who decides when a project should be phased out or redirected into new channels? No matter how your parish is structured, you will want to establish clear-cut procedures for defining a particular program's goal, assigning responsibility for its planning and execution and for its periodic evaluation.

Other questions concern the importance and meaning a program has for those who are asked to carry it out. Are their targets clearly understood and capable of achievement? Are your committee members directly concerned with a successful outcome, or are they asked to perform perfunctory tasks with little visible impact? Personal antagonisms can destroy a sense of direction and demand a chairman's utmost tact. The same chairman must somehow contrive to keep the committee members alert by giving them a full measure of satisfaction, even excitement, if their motivation is not to falter.

These are only some of the factors that influence the daily operation of your parish. You will think of others and will discover even more as you become more deeply involved. And now for systems of parish organization.

Committee System

Under the Committee System arrangement the different functions of parish life are divided among separate committees, each under the chairmanship of a well-qualified person with some skill in his or her assigned field, who may or may not be a member of the vestry. In this form of organization, committee members are frequently named by the rector and often assume a high degree of independence in their group's affairs. Some committees, such as finance and property maintenance, may report directly to the vestry. Others—worship, music, Christian education, and youth, for example—to the rector. And still others, such as the Episcopal Churchwomen and laymen's groups, to the annual meeting of the parish.

While this type of organization allows free play to the committee members' talents and imagination, the lines of authority may be so loosely drawn that coordinated planning becomes difficult and communication between the committees themselves and the vestry seriously threatened. It is a rare rector who can single-handedly keep track of each committee's activities and manage to impose a sense of common purpose and joint planning that will tie the various programs together in a unified approach.

Council System

The Council System provides that the management of parish affairs is shared by the vestry and a council composed of representatives from each program group in the parish. The vestry, in this case, concerns itself with fiscal management and setting general policy directives on the basis of recommendations submitted to it by the council. Through its subsidiary committees, the council carries out the parish program. As a vestry member, you may or may not serve on the council, although someone from the vestry should be a member of each of the committees that makes up the council.

The council chairman is appointed by your rector, with the approval of the vestry. Council members may also be appointed by the rector, who may activate new committees as the need arises and dissolve or consolidate those already in existence. Council meetings are ordinarily open to any member of the parish who wants to attend, so that there is an opportunity for everyone to take part in the parish's planning and evaluation. It is wise to rotate the committee chairmanships from time to time to gain broader participation by the congregation.

Committees of the council are similar in nature to those of the Committee System above and, depending on the interest of your parish, might also include ecumenical relations, social relations, community affairs, special events, and stewardship. The Council System can successfully involve many parishioners in many programs, but also carries with it the seeds of misunderstanding or competition between vestry and council, so that a close working relationship may not be easy to sustain.

Commission System

Of the four traditional patterns for parish organization, the Commission System offers considerable scope for personal contribution by parishioners and the assumption of direct responsibility by each member of the vestry.

The principal areas of parish activity are assigned to separate commissions, each under the chairmanship of a vestry member appointed jointly by the vestry and the rector. All of the vestry are members of at least one commission. The chairmen invite parishioners of special competence and skills to join their groups, which are charged with planning, implementing, and periodically reviewing their particular parts of the general program. Depending on the nature of their assignments, chairmen can enlist the aid of growing numbers of men and women on subcommittees as their projects catch hold and gain momentum.

Because each commission is headed by a vestry member, you receive a comprehensive, up-to-the-minute review of the entire parish operation at each vestry meeting, when the chairmen make their reports. Responsibility and leadership are vested in the parish's elected representatives, the vestry members, who become better acquainted with other members of the congregation and, as they work side by side on the commission, are in an excellent position to talk and to listen.

Task Force System

The Task Force System form of organization closely approximates the Commission System except that the task forces are activated for a limited time only, to accomplish a particular piece of work. Each task force's membership is open to any parishioner who wants to join, and it is wise to arrange to have at least one vestry member belong to each group so that communication between task forces and vestry is easy and open. This system is particularly useful when a parish is eager to carry out simultaneously several programs or projects with widely diverse aims.

Several parishes have enlarged the prerogatives of the vestry's executive committee, so that it now meets monthly, in advance of regular vestry meetings, to examine problems that need attention and to recommend action to the full vestry. This relieves the vestry itself from time-consuming attention to detail and frees it to concentrate on one or two major topics that the leadership group suggests for its agenda. To work well, such an arrangement assumes a constant flow of information to executive committee members and a strong degree of trust between them and the full vestry.

Countless variations may be rung on these themes, and parishes borrow freely from each of the four prototypes in designing the system best suited to their own interests. The wise vestry will recognize that a well-knit table of organization which fits together logically on paper may simply not work when launched on the unpredictable seas of parish life, and will build into its system some provision for flexibility.

Leadership entails risk: you will have to decide how tight a control should be exercised over every facet of parish life and whether new interests and ideas may flourish within the parish, but outside its formal structure. Some years ago in several Southern congregations, for example, civil rights groups were organized that had no official status, but were an important part of some parishioners' mission.

In recent years newer organizational shapes have made a tentative appearance. One diocese, for instance, is considering a proposal that as few as ten men and women who want to constitute themselves a congregation be given formal recognition and representation in its diocesan convention. More innovations of this sort will no doubt emerge in the near future as small parishes experiment further with the services of the non-stipendiary clergy in working out a viable life style for themselves. What you will want to look for is the assurance that your parish's personal and professional talent, both lay and clerical, is being used to optimum advantage and that sooner or later every willing parishioner will have the opportunity to serve.

VI

Your Annual Parish Meeting

The principal purpose of your parish's annual meeting, as defined by canon law, is to elect members of the vestry to replace those whose terms have just expired. But with careful planning it can also become a major occasion in the parish year for rallying morale, analyzing the progress of the past twelve months, and concentrating on your goals for the immediate future.

In larger parishes, the rector usually appoints the wardens, several vestry members, and parishioners to a nominating committee. It is their duty to present nominees who will bring additional know-how to the vestry, so that its membership will reflect a broad spectrum of expertise ranging from the legal and fiscal to such fields as communications, teaching, social work, and the women of the parish. Many nominating committees prepare a slate of more names than there are positions to be filled, to offer a choice to the parishioners and to forestall any embarrassment among the losers. A person's commitment to the parish merits consideration in determining his or her qualifications, and each one should also be sounded out about his or her willingness to serve.

The rotating vestry has become increasingly popular in recent years. The vestry is divided into classes, each of which serves for a specified period, usually three years. When a vestry member's term expires, or in some parishes when he has served two terms, he or she is ineligible for reelection for one year. This has the obvious advantage of opening the vestry to wider membership over a period of time and also rotates off some members who may not be so effective as those who replace them. It also means that periodically you lose the knowledge of experienced members.

In some parishes it is customary to supplement the nominating committee's list by making nominations from the floor of the meeting. Others provide that this be done in advance, by petition with a prescribed number of signatures. Whatever procedure is followed, you will want to make sure, if you are asked to serve on the nominating committee, that your candidates know what election to the vestry will mean in terms of their time, energy, and imagination. A few congregations with a high degree of turnover among their parishioners solve the problem of how to bring new members rapidly into the mainstream of parish life by drawing lots for a number of their nominees, which has succeeded remarkably well because these candidates know beforehand what is involved in serving on the vestry.

The canon law of your diocese states who is eligible to vote for vestry members—usually anyone above a certain age who has attended church regularly and pledged support during the past year—and your parish bylaws stipulate how many new members are to be chosen each year, as well as whether a warden is to be elected at the same time. Since state law in most dioceses requires that the polls be kept open for an hour, you are presented with a rare opportunity for a sixty-minute dialogue with interested members of the parish after the ballots have been distributed.

This is an excellent time for questioning, probing, and perhaps revising the goals your parish sets for itself. You and your colleagues on the vestry may want to ask those present to comment on the job descriptions that have been written for your clergy. What better occasion could be found to announce plans for a new parish program or to express appreciation to retiring committee chairmen while introducing their successors at the same time? New members of the congregation can be formally welcomed. A program committee that has had notable success can explain why. Perhaps another committee can ask for suggestions to improve its work. A debate between opposing points of view on a particular project, preconceived to an extent that does not rob it of spontaneity, is a surefire means of arous-ing interest and awareness. You have the alert attention of this mini-congregation for at least sixty minutes and can make of it what you will.

An imaginative planning committee can overcome the dead-weight of statistics-filled reports by devices such as these and could also plan the agenda around a pleasant meal. Even with only a comparative handful of parishioners present, assuming that they constitute a quorum for voting purposes, your meeting can be hugely successful if the participants are enthusiastically moved to action. Think, for a moment, of what you would like to say to a dedicated portion of your congregation and what you would like to hear from them in the way of commitment. And then act.

VII

Calling a Rector

Whataever hen the time comes for your rector to retire or to accept a call to another parish, your sense of loss or secret relief at his or her departure will be compounded by dismay over your parish's uncertain future. But every congregation sooner or later passes through such an upheaval and discovers much that is helpful in the Church's practice and customs for finding a new rector.

Each diocese has its own canon law, and frequently its own set of written procedures, to supplement the sparse provisions of national Canon 23 of Title III, "Of the Filling of Vacant Cures." The national canon, quoted in full in the appendix, states that your wardens are to notify the bishop that the parish is vacant and arrange with him for someone to conduct services in your rector's absence. The canon also says that, when you have selected a new rector, you must notify the bishop. If he does not object to your choice within thirty days, you are free to elect as rector the person you have chosen. A written notice of the election, signed by your wardens, must then be sent to the bishop to be entered in the official records of the diocese.

If there is to be an interval between the departure of your present rector and the institution of his successor—and strong arguments can be made for a six- or twelve-month interval to permit the preparation of a careful self-study of the parish that will be useful in calling your new rector—it is better that your supply priest or interim pastor not be a candidate for the vacancy. During this period the vestry, and especially the wardens, must be prepared to step into the departing rector's shoes insofar as possible, to prevent a loss of momentum or even the collapse of parish programs with which he has been closely identified. You will discover that many members of the congregation will exert themselves to take up the slack in this unusual period and do more than their share to keep wheels turning.

The first question in everyone's mind will be: How do we find another person who will not only fit in with our parish, but exert the special sort of spiritual leadership we need? It is this question which the national canon has sidestepped, leaving it to the dioceses to fill in the particulars, and, while there may be differences in detail, the broad outlines of the procedure for calling a rector vary but slightly from one diocese to another.

Your first action as a vestry will probably be to make arrangements for writing a detailed, up-to-date profile of your parish that articulates its goals and strengths, its weaknesses and the measures being taken to overcome them, its special programs, and the parts to be played by rector and congregation in each. It is here that your communications pipelines with the parishioners will prove of inestimable value. If you have already drawn up a self-study as suggested above, it will need only to be polished and made current.

Some dioceses require that your profile of parish needs be further refined into three subsidiary categories: a goals description, a job description of the new rector's duties, and a personnel description of the sort of person you are looking for. Your parishioners' views are of paramount importance in phrasing each of these statements.

Simultaneously with preparing the parish profile, your vestry will want to appoint a search committee, consisting of your wardens, several vestry members, and representatives from women's and young people's groups and other important segments of the parish at large. It is to this committee that names of possible candidates will be suggested by your parishioners and by others who will hear of the vacancy and want to mention clergy they esteem. The search committee is also responsible for maintaining close liaison with your bishop during the entire process.

It is important for your search committee members to understand the steps they will be taking and the sequence they will follow. Most committees try to keep the whole congregation fully informed as each progressive stage is reached, for the business of finding a new rector is a concern shared by each one of them.

A number of dioceses have diocesan deployment officers on their staffs who can be of enormous help to search committees in their work. From time to time a vestry may also authorize its search committee to retain the services of a clergy placement bureau, a private firm that specializes in helping to bring the right person to the attention of an appropriate parish.

While organizing the search committee, it may be advisable for several members of the vestry to request an appointment with the bishop to discuss the parish's specific needs. He will want a concise description of your congregation's current expectations, as well as your plans for the parish's future, which will be readily at hand in the parish profile.

A primary resource and the official source of names for parish vacancies is the Church Deployment Office of our Church*, which was established in 1969 to build a national data bank of information about Episcopal clergy based on detailed questionnaires that were sent to all the ordained clergy. This office is equipped to suggest candidates with any given combination of training and experience that may be called for by your job description and can also provide information about the backgrounds of particular clergy in whom you are interested. It responds to requests from dioceses, so that, once your criteria have been established, your inquiry must be channeled through your bishop's office.

* See appendix.

The Church Deployment Office has prepared two leaflets on this subject: "Interviewing in the Calling Process" and "Caring for Clergy in the Calling Process," both of which make helpful suggestions for the search committee's guidance. They may be obtained from the Deployment Office at 815 Second Avenue, New York, N.Y. 10017.

The size, the location, or the peculiar nature of your parish may cause you to look seriously at a non-stipendiary member of the clergy, who would not devote his full time or energies to the position of rector because he earns his living elsewhere, but whose native gifts could nevertheless offer dynamic leadership to your congregation. For a variety of compelling reasons, some bishops are strongly committed to the steady development of the non-stipendiary ministry. If you are interested, ask your bishop.

Before commencing any detailed investigation of the candidates suggested to your search committee, it is customary in most dioceses for their names to be submitted to your bishop for his evaluation. After conferring with his staff, your bishop will send you a recommended list of names, which will probably include some of yours and some new ones as well.

It is at this stage that the search committee will begin exhaustive inquiries into the nominees' backgrounds. But first, to avoid putting any of your candidates in an embarrassing situation, you will be well advised to find out if they might be interested in the position. In some dioceses the bishop's nominations must be considered before those from other sources; it is wise to look them over carefully in any case. His principal interest, like yours, is to put your parish in the capable hands of a cleric singularly well suited to the position. He has access to a good deal of information not generally available, so that his advice is not to be shrugged off lightly.

The scope of the investigation will be determined largely by the amount of time and money available. Each candidate under serious scrutiny should be studied painstakingly from the viewpoint of his or her effectiveness as the possible rector of your parish, with particular attention to his experience and past career. The more people you can speak to about him—and speaking is preferable to writing—the more sharply defined will be your assessment of his abilities and deficiencies.

Sooner or later your search committee will want to interview its top candidates and will need to know exactly what is being offered in terms of salary, housing allowance, insurance premiums, and the like. Once these points have been mentioned— and they may not come up at first—the candidate will want to discuss the sort of parish you are and what you expect from a new rector. How much of the parish program is shouldered by the laity? What freedom would he or she have in introducing new projects or changing those already in motion? How much support could he expect from the parish? the outside community? At the same time your representatives will want to explore the candidate's ideas about the ministry and his concept of the role of parish rector: preacher, counselor, teacher, activist, evangelist, or a combination of each?

An appointment should be arranged, if possible, to visit the candidate in his or her parish, meet the family and listen to a sermon. Every effort should also be made during this exploratory visit to speak with responsible members of the community, both from within and outside the candidate's parish. How does he spend his time? Are he and his family well known and liked in the neighborhood? Does he work well with clergy of other faiths? Is he an inspiring leader?

Distance may prevent such visits, but the committee will want, at the barest minimum, to hear a candidate's sermon. He could be invited to preach at a neighboring parish at your expense. It is neither usual nor wise to invite a nominee to take the service in your vacant parish.

After the interviews a vestry sometimes asks the candidate to put into writing his or her concept of what the parish needs and wants from a new rector, what he considers its strengths and weaknesses, and how he sees himself and the vestry working together in their new relationships. The discussion and clarification that follows is the first mutual review of roles and expectations that can be made part of the contractual agreement if he is called.

The national canon leaves it to the diocese to decide whether the vestry or a special meeting of the parish should elect a new rector. When the search committee has completed its studies, its findings are submitted to the vestry or to the parish with any recommendations it may choose to make, for reasoned and deliberate discussion before voting on the nominees. When a person has been chosen, his or her name is forwarded to the bishop for approval. If your bishop disapproves, another meeting of the vestry or the parish must be called to consider his opposition. Nothing in canon law prevents your overriding his objections, but it goes without saying that your bishop's grounds for disapproval should be most carefully explored.

Once a new rector has been elected, your vestry will constitute one of its members to present your offer to him or her in writing—in letter-of-agreement form, as described in Chapter II—with explicit mention of salary, automobile and housing allowances, insurance and retirement benefits, and other contractual obligations, such as provision for a mutual annual performance review. On the receipt of the nominee's written acceptance of your call, a formal notice to your bishop signed by both wardens completes the procedure. Of course if the person you have called declines, the process must be continued until a rector has been elected and accepts.

National canon law (III, 21, Sec. 1-b) requires that assistant ministers in a parish serve "under the authority and direction of the Rector." It goes on to state that such ministers—regardless of the title given them: curate, associate, etc.—"may not serve beyond the period of service of the Rector." The vestry, however, has the right to request such a person, or persons, to remain in service until the new rector has been called, "under such conditions as the Bishop and Vestry shall determine." This is a matter that will have received previous attention from everyone concerned—rector, curate, bishop, and vestry. Each will probably want the curate's job description to be recast and brought up to date if he or she is invited to remain, which may involve a new letter of agreement specifying duties and assignments. Since the parish's professional staff is also employed by the rector, he has the option of retaining any of them or of finding replacements.

One other national canon deserves mention. Title III, Canon 22, "Of the Dissolution of the Pastoral Relation," states unequivocally that, "a Rector may not resign his Parish without the consent of the said Parish." In other words, if you insist that your rector stay with you, canon law backs you up. It is a rare parish that would hold a person against his will, but this technicality might open the door to an entirely new relationship if you can persuade your rector that your parish offers a greater challenge and satisfaction.

The same canon outlines the steps to be followed if either the rector or the body that elected him "shall desire a separation and dissolution of the pastoral relation, and the parties be not agreed respecting a separation and dissolution." Either one may give written notice of dissatisfaction to the bishop, who, after consultation with the Standing Committee of the diocese, "shall be the ultimate arbiter and judge." His decision that the pastoral relation shall cease or that it shall continue is final and binding on both sides.

VIII

Every Member Canvass

If a survey were made of the thousands of canvasses conducted throughout the Church each year, no two would be found exactly alike in every respect. All share a minimum goal of raising funds for the parish program in the year ahead, and all seek to accomplish this through the willing support of their congregations. But aside from the same starting point and finish line, the paths these canvasses pursue wind through terrain so much of their own making that it has few identifying features for others to follow.

Without attempting to plot the ideal course for a canvass, let us examine five key factors that together will strongly influence its likelihood of eventual success.

Leadership

The caliber and the character of those who lead the canvass can be crucial to its outcome. Because of its familiarity—asking the same people to do the same thing at the same time of year—the canvass could assume the dreary nature of a necessary but monotonous chore that must somehow be slogged through every twelve months. If this is how it appears to those who take part, and through them infects every member of the parish, the opportunity for significant breakthrough in terms of result or understanding will almost certainly be stillborn.

The need for resourceful leadership is thus doubly urgent, not only to reach the monetary goal, but also to shake off the dust of former years in devising a fresh approach that will capture the imagination of those involved and propel them into action.

How these leaders are chosen is a matter of local preference. In some parishes the canvass chairman is always a member of the vestry, but the choice should logically fall on the best qualified man or woman to be found and not on the parish office he or she may happen to hold.

The leaders will want to build their campaign strategy, its organization and timetable, on what has worked well in other parishes as well as their own, while improvising new techniques to make the canvass more effective. Some dioceses now issue a detailed set of instructions on the model canvass, which suggest a step-by-step procedure for building your committee structure and a timetable for carrying out its activities, week by week. One such plan stresses continuing consultation between the rector and the canvass' general chairman and provides for committees on stewardship, on planning for the parish's next ten years, on communications, youth, the enlistment of canvassers, on arranging that every parishioner be visited and that every canvasser make his or her pledge in advance. You would be well advised to get in touch with your diocesan office to see if it can give you such information.

In recent years the practice of tithing—giving one-tenth or more of one's income to the Church—has slowly won acceptance. The Diocese of Alabama has spearheaded this concept, and its Alabama Plan has been considered and adopted in many other parts of the country. The plan works simply enough: before asking your congregation to tithe, the rector and each member of the vestry must solemnly pledge at least ten percent of their incomes to the parish. With such forceful impetus behind it, the idea can be presented persuasively to your parishioners in a way that will quite transform your canvass results. Detailed information about the plan, as well as the help of a consultant to start it, may be obtained from the office of the Bishop of Alabama at 521 North 20th Street, Birmingham, AL 35203.

Official approval of this practice was given by the General Convention of 1982, which called upon all Episcopalians to join in "accepting the biblical tithe as the minimum standard of Christian giving."

Other parishes use an approach known as proportionate giving, which asks members of the congregation to consider their pledges as an act of thanksgiving, offering in gratitude to God a portion of what He has given to every one of us. Here again the vestry subscribes to the plan before it is brought to the parish, each one considering what percentage of his or her gross income will be shared with God through faithful stewardship of His blessings.

Once this concept has been accepted, the vestry suggests that each member of the parish choose a fixed percentage of income as his or her pledge. This can be illustrated by a chart showing what weekly contributions would be in terms of various percentages of annual gross income. No particular percentage is suggested; this is left to the individual to decide, alone with his or her conscience.

Pattern of Giving

A parish, as has become increasingly clear, is more than anything else the men, women, and children who come together in worship and thanksgiving. And just as it would be a dangerous half-truth to equate their commitment to the Church with dollars alone, so is it misleading to view the annual canvass as purely a means to balance the budget.

Parishioners already give of themselves: some, of their time and talents to the work of the parish, others solely of their devotion on Sunday mornings. The canvass may be used to extend these gifts of time and skill into financial commitments, but not at the expense of overlooking the other ways in which so many contribute to the life of the parish. Rather, it might well attempt to fuse the many into one by seeking to enlist each member's financial support at the same time as it invites the member to participate more fully in any parish program he or she finds congenial.

Once each year a group of canvassers calls on other parishioners. The message the canvassers take with them will have a profound effect on how these others see the parish in months to come. Will it be in terms of cash alone or as an opportunity for many forms of service and fulfillment?

Pledging

The parish budget, sometimes prepared in advance of the canvass, presumably contains every item of foreseeable expense for the coming year, including funds the parish plans to contribute to outside causes on the local, diocesan, and national scenes, as well as a reserve for contingencies. The canvass' immediate purpose is to secure pledges of a sufficient amount to balance the budget after allowance has been made for such other sources of income as plate offerings and any special contributions that may be anticipated.

If your projected budget shows a sizable increase or if the number of contributors has declined, your canvass committee may opt to seek an across-the-board percentage increase in the size of every pledge to make up the difference. If your parish wants to sponsor a new day-care center, for example, or underwrite a hospital chaplaincy for the first time in addition to other program commitments, the pledges will have to reflect the added expense.

The mechanics of designing, printing, distributing, filing, and following up on the pledge cards themselves, whether by letter or another visit, should be carefully planned and assigned to responsible committee members or others within the parish. In some dioceses you can get excellent advice on how to prepare and handle these forms from the person on your bishop's staff who has been specially trained for stewardship work. Even if you are satisfied that processing the pledge cards and mailings is handled smoothly in your parish, he or she is well worth consulting.

Opinions differ about publicizing a fixed dollar goal and about setting the goal at a higher figure than the canvass is expected to produce. Both methods have been tried, and neither offers an ironclad guarantee of 100 percent response. One prime fund-raising rule not to be overlooked is that the canvassers should already have made their own pledges and, ideally, each canvass-er's pledge should represent a substantial increase over the year before. Matching canvassers with persons of comparable financial standing may make it easier for them to speak more openly about the amounts they have pledged.

How these pledges are secured will influence decisively the amount of money the canvass will provide.

There is a world of difference between asking a number of canvassers to visit a few parishioners at home, where they pass the time of day and then leave a pledge card, and sending out a goup of trained enthusiasts, eager to describe the parish's activities and to discuss the rationale for each item in a budget that has already been outlined in a previous mailing. Your canvass chairman and the members of the canvass committee will decide how detailed their advance preparations should be and whether they might include several preliminary letters or a meeting of the whole parish.

An interesting development of comparatively recent origin is the emergence of a second, complementary canvass several months after the principal effort has been completed. This may be prompted by an unexpected need for new program funds or by the failure of the regular canvass to finance normal expenses. It could duplicate the original effort in structure and organiza-tion, or it could take capsule form, such as asking each parishio-ner for a special offering every day in Lent. Parishes with highly mobile congregations sometimes approach in the spring newcomers who have arrived since the completion of the regular fall canvass.

Training

To act as your emissaries—and the role of canvasser is a direct extension of your fiscal responsibility as vestry member—the canvassers should be prepared to discuss intelligently the general programs of the parish and the funds allocated to each part. The depth of their training depends on the campaign strategy adopted by your chairman and his or her lieutenants. If the canvass is to be anything but a gentle exercise in the social graces, the canvassers will need thorough indoctrination on the parish budget and financial position, as well as the opportunities the parish faces. They should probably be armed with a printed set of facts and figures to help them answer questions easily.

Many parishes now place greater emphasis on year-round stewardship, constantly re-examining their goals and reshaping their programs to take full advantage of the time and abilities volunteered by members of the congregation. When this process has been buttressed by continuing, two-way communication between vestry and congregation, canvassers will no longer start from scratch. They will already be familiar with much of what goes on in the parish and, what is even more pertinent, so will the people they visit.

These same parishes sometimes conduct their canvasses before preparing a budget, so that instead of being asked to pledge toward a budget that is already complete in every detail, the congregations are invited to contribute from their total resources to advance the work of the parish in the community and the world. If the parish's internal and external challenges are clearly understood, the response to a pre-budget canvass can be magnificent.

While the use of printed material is a valuable training aid, it is no substitute for the spoken word at indoctrination sessions. In some parishes all the canvassers meet, perhaps for a meal, to hear the chairman outline his or her plans and the treasurer explain the budget. In other parishes they gather in smaller groups to examine the previous pledges of persons they are to visit. But why limit attendance to canvassers alone? Every parishioner has a personal stake in the outcome and may have suggestions or criticism well worth listening to.

Person-to-Person Contact
The crux of the canvass is, of course, the conversation between canvasser and parishioner. Parish bulletins usually carry notices of the date of the canvass for several weeks before it takes place, and a general mailing will probably have alerted the congregation that it is coming. Your callers may want to write or telephone the parishioners they are to visit to make sure they will be at home and also to introduce themselves.

The nature of the visits will already have been shaped by the training given your canvassers, who will be equipped to discuss parish affairs just as fully as—but no more than—they have been briefed to do.

No matter how well informed the canvassers may be, however, the canvass is primarily an occasion for members of the congregation to meet each other and talk of their common interest in the parish. How they choose to express this interest in their pledges will hinge on their awareness of purposeful movement within the parish and their desire to take an active part in its progress.

IX

Capital Funds and Planned Giving

A clear distinction must be made at the outset between capital funds raised for a specific purpose, such as building a parish hall or putting a new roof on the church, and those sought for a parish endowment. The entire concept of an endowment has been scrutinized carefully in recent years; it will be examined more closely at the end of this chapter, in connection with planned giving.

As soon as vestry members begin to agree that a major project with a price tag well beyond the means of the parish budget should be looked at seriously, the time has come to ask a small *ad hoc* committee to do just that. In its preliminary deliberation, the group will ask itself: Is this essential, or can we get along without it? How far does it go to meet the spiritual, as well as the practical needs of the parish? Will it be sufficiently appealing to arouse a satisfactory response from the congregation without diverting attention from other, more pressing financial needs that may arise in the near future? In other words, "Does it make sense to go all out for this project now?"

Concurrently with this questioning, the committee will want

to secure a firm estimate of all expenses involved, which, if a campaign is to be mounted, would also include charges for secretarial time, the preparation and printing of materials for publicity and communication, and any professional counsel that may be necessary. The total of these costs will represent the campaign's tentative dollar goal.

Armed with the costs, the *ad hoc* group may want at this point to invite a number of parishioners or the members of one family to underwrite the project themselves, perhaps as a memorial to a relative. They will also no doubt want to inquire from the diocesan office whether other parishes have contemplated similar action and, if so, to confer with those who supervised the fund raising. The diocesan official responsible for stewardship can be especially helpful in the planning stages by pointing out pitfalls to be skirted and with technical advice that only experience can give.

The national Church's Office of Stewardship* maintains a resource list of printed materials on stewardship and will be glad to send you a copy. The Office also has a record of professional stewardship consultants throughout the country: you may want to confer with one of them before making any detailed plans and perhaps contract for his or her services as consultant during your campaign.

If your project has to do with a building program, you will want to know that two national agencies make loans for such purposes. They are the Episcopal Church Building Fund and The Episcopal Church Foundation, both listed in the appendix.

One last bridge must be crossed before the final decision is made to launch the campaign: a searching scrutiny of the parish's giving potential. Your rector, your treasurer, your stewardship chairman, and your canvass chairman can shed light on the matter, which is of direct concern to each one of them, particularly insofar as it affects normal contributions to the parish in

---

* See appendix.

the months ahead. If they and others you consult agree that your congregation has the ability to support this project above and beyond its financial commitment to regular program, you are ready to move.

The mention of the stewardship chairman just above implies that your parish has set up a stewardship program to mobilize the talents and energies of your parishioners all year long and not just for the Every Member Canvass or a capital funds campaign. Your canvass chairman will of course be a noteworthy member of the stewardship team, which, however, has a broader interest than just fund raising.

The committee structure for a major gifts campaign, like that of the canvass, can be as intricate or as simple as your situation demands. A good rule of thumb is to build your organization sparingly, always remembering that communication is the life-blood of every endeavor in which many people are engaged.

The principal difference between a capital funds drive and the Every Member Canvass, aside from their respective purposes, is that the former raises the bulk of its funds from a very few contributors, while the canvass ordinarily shows a more even distribution among its donors of the amounts they give. To persuade less than 5 per cent of your donors to contribute between 80 and 90 per cent of your goal, you must know not only who they are and how to interest them in your cause, but, even more critical, how much you want them to give. Setting too high or too low a figure or settling for less than they can reasonably be expected to give can unbalance the whole effort. The campaign will rise or fall on the abilities of a handful of men and women to determine the potential of your major gifts prospects and to secure pledges of their support before the drive is publicly announced.

An effective way to secure major sums is through the use of planned giving. Committee members and those who solicit major gifts should have easy access to information on current tax laws and the use of trusts or the various options for planned giving, so that they may answer questions or work out a plan suited to the donor's individual circumstances or convenience.

When the major gifts phase of your campaign is well in hand according to the timetable laid down in advance, you are ready to speak to, write to, and call on the rest of the parish. Matching the person asking for a pledge with a prospect in the same financial bracket is even more desirable here than in your Every Member Canvass because so much more is at stake. Visual aids and leaflets can be used to great advantage in acquainting the parish with the urgency of your project and explaining the benefits it will bring with it. Your experienced canvassers can help with arrangements for visiting each parishioner and processing the pledges, as well as in alerting the general committee to any areas that need special attention as the campaign gains momentum.

Leadership, planning, the continuing exchange of progress reports, and, ultimately, the words of one person to another: all are vital. Each will help to spark a sense of working together enthusiastically for the common good that is the distinguishing characteristic of a lively parish.

Raising capital for a parish endowment is a decidedly different undertaking. Many men and women who want to continue supporting their churches indefinitely have written into their wills a bequest to their parish, the income from which will match their annual contributions while living. The Book of Common Prayer urges all of us to do this by stating,

The Minister of the Congregation is directed to instruct the people, from time to time, about the duty of Christian parents to make prudent provision for the well-being of their families, and of all persons to make wills, while they are in health, arranging for the disposal of their temporal goods, not neglecting, if they are able, to leave bequests for religious and charitable uses. (Page 445)

You, as a member of the vestry, must help to decide how these bequests and the parish endowment are to be used: whether they will only assure that your church remains open or whether they open the door to a vibrant, imaginative expression of your congregation's interest in the world.

If you choose to consider the return from endowment as ordinary parish income for budgetary purposes, it will have an effect on the level of contributions and commitment from your congregation. In the center of some cities today can be found handsome churches, many of them well maintained and architectural landmarks, but with dying congregations. Granted that their plight has been aggravated by shifts of population and represents an extreme, without endowments they would have been forced to follow their parishioners to new locations or merge with neighboring parishes in the same situation, adapting themselves gracefully to new life styles.

In vivid contrast stand those parishes which put all bequests to immediate use in current programs or which set them aside as special funds to be used outside the parish. They may adopt a struggling parish in a nearby city, sharing man- and woman-power as well as dollars, or they may concentrate their endowment income in any one of several mission areas. Many of these same congregations also share their pledged income fifty-fifty, spending half on running the parish and the other half on outreach.

If you have already formed a stewardship committee, as suggested in the previous chapter, its members can play an important part in building the parish endowment. Or your vestry and rector may prefer to retain for themselves the direction of this effort. In any case, you will want to consider ways to encourage contributions to the endowment, together with a clear-cut statement about how such gifts will be used.

These approaches include not only bequests, but also gifts of life insurance, trusts, a pooled income fund, and gift annuities, to name the most frequently used. You will need the advice of tax lawyers and trust officers and, if you decide to spread your nets that wide, of insurance brokers and real estate people from the congregation or the community.

You and your fellow vestry members will want to investigate the legal requirements imposed by state law in organizing any of these plans and make sure that they have been satisfied.

One effective means of bringing such a program before the parish is the estate planning seminar, at which experts in the fields of tax laws, trusts, insurance and real estate can discuss the importance of estate planning. Your diocese may be able to help you organize this sort of meeting, and the national Church's Office of Stewardship, listed in the appendix, has a trained officer who will be glad to answer questions about arranging the seminar and to provide supporting material.

However you decide to proceed, the results will only become apparent over a period of years.

If your parish is a small one without many well-to-do members, some of the foregoing may seem superfluous or beyond your reach. But with imagination and hard work, the basic principles can be made to apply to any situation.

No one knows why one person writes the parish into his or her will while someone in the next pew never does. It must be assumed that somewhere in the donor's relationship with fellow parishioners, with the clergy or with the life of the parish, something spoke and made him or her one of a larger family. The donor's bequest cements this relationship for all time.

X

The Episcopal Church

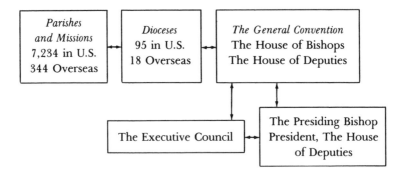

According to the 1982 edition of The Episcopal Church Annual, there are 3,037,420 baptized Episcopalians, of whom 2,018,870 are communicants in good standing, meaning that they attend church regularly.

The Church Pension Fund listed 12,720 Episcopal clergy as of March 31, 1982, including 258 bishops. Of the total, 8,164 are engaged in the active ministry and employed by the Church, 2,522 are retired, and 2,034 secularly employed.

Annual conventions of the ninety-five dioceses in the United States carry out routine business, write diocesan canon law, and elect their bishops. The eighteen dioceses overseas are similarly governed. In addition, the Convocation of American Churches in Europe, with six parishes and missions in France, Germany, Italy, and Switzerland, is under the jurisdiction of the Presiding Bishop, with a bishop in charge; for organizational purposes, it is usually referred to as a diocese as well.

The General Convention meets every three years and is the ultimate source of authority in the Church. It consists of two houses: the House of Bishops with 258 members has the Presiding Bishop as chairman *ex officio* and a vice-chairman elected from the membership; the House of Deputies, with 904 members, elects its own president and vice-president. The latter House is composed of the four clerical and four lay deputies who are elected by diocesan conventions in each domestic and overseas diocese and the Convocation of American Churches in Europe. Some dioceses do not send their full complements of deputies so that those present usually number less than 904.

The General Convention is assisted and counseled by 27 Joint Committees, Commissions, Boards, and Agencies. Some of the counseling agencies have permanent status at the pleasure of the Convention; others are of a more temporary nature.

The Executive Council's forty members are bishops, clergy, and lay persons elected by the General Convention and, two each, by the nine Provinces, which are regional groupings of dioceses. It is the interim governing body of the Church between General Conventions and derives its authority from the General Convention. The Presiding Bishop serves as President and Chairman of the Executive Council and the President of the House of Deputies as Vice-Chairman. The Executive Council has six Standing Committees and, as of 1982, twelve Special, Advisory and *Ad Hoc* Committees. The Executive Council currently has a staff of some one hundred ten men and women at The Episcopal Church Center, 815 Second Avenue, New York City, who maintain liaison with the dioceses and carry out the program functions of the General Convention, subject to the direction of the Council.

The Presiding Bishop is elected by the House of Bishops from among its membership, subject to confirmation by the House of Deputies. He must resign his own diocese when he assumes his new office, or within the next six months. He is elected for a term of twelve years or until the Convention after his sixty-fifth birthday. In addition to his administrative duties, he is chief pastor, primate, and spokesman for the Church.

The president of the House of Deputies is elected by that body from among its membership at an early stage of a given General Convention. The president-elect takes office at that Convention's adjournment and serves through the succeeding General Convention. An incumbent president may be reelected twice, to serve for a term of nine successive years in all. If the president is a lay person, the vice-president is elected from the ranks of the clergy and vice versa.

Appendix I

Resources

Diocesan Office _____ Phone:_____
                  _____
                  _____

Your Bishop: _____ Phone:_____
                  _____
                  _____

Diocesan
Treasurer: _____ Phone:_____
                  _____
                  _____

Chancellor
of the Diocese: _____ Phone:_____
(Legal Counsel) _____
                  _____

Diocesan   _____ Phone:_____
Committees   _____ Phone:_____
                  _____ Phone:_____

The Alban Institute
The Rev. Loren B. Mead,
Director
Mount St. Alban
Washington, DC 20016

An international research and development organization, focusing on congregational life through research, consulting, and problem-solving. Publishes papers on the results and other pertinent topics.

Center for Parish
Development
The Rev. Paul Dietrich,
Executive Director
208 East Fifth Street
Naperville, IL 60540

Wide range of services available in leadership development, stewardship cultivation, strategic and operational planning, program measurement and development in response to needs, transition management and performance planning and evaluation.

The Church
Deployment Office
The Rev. Roddey Reid, Jr.,
Executive Director
William A. Thompson,
J.D., Associate Director
815 Second Avenue
New York, NY 10017

This office supplies personal profiles to parishes, dioceses, and other institutions wishing to employ clergy or church professional workers. In addition, lists of position openings are circulated to dioceses and clergy.

Episcopal Church Building
Fund
The Rev. Sherrill Scales,
Jr., Executive Vice-
President
815 Second Avenue
New York, NY 10017

Provides two-fold service of planning and financing construction, improvement, or repair of church buildings through interest-bearing loans (loans up to $35,000 are made against promissory notes).

The Episcopal Church
 Foundation
Frederick L. Redpath,
 Executive Vice-President
815 Second Avenue
New York, NY 10017

A national, independent organization of lay men and women which makes grants to projects to benefit the clergy and strengthen the parish, as well as for theological education and communications; which makes loans for church construction and awards fellowships for doctoral study to recent seminary graduates.

The Executive Council
 of The Episcopal Church
The Rt. Rev. John M.
 Allin, Presiding Bishop
815 Second Avenue
New York, NY 10017

Education for Mission and Ministry Office
Resources for lay ministry, education, evangelism, youth, three Black Episcopal colleges, and military chaplaincies.

National Mission in Church and Society Office
Responsible for coordinating and administering a wide variety of programs and relationships with the Church's 14 domestic aided dioceses; its ethnic and Appalachian ministries; its ministries to the aging and the deaf; its grants for programs addressing human needs and social justice; its cooperation with dioceses and congregations on social, economic, and moral issues; and its representation in Washington.

World Mission Office

Partnership with 16 Anglican Provinces overseas, as well as support for 19 overseas Episcopal dioceses; missionary support; cooperation with ecumenical agencies and furthering the ecumenical efforts of The Episcopal Church; support for the Church's participation in Third World development projects.

Office of Communication

Initiates, develops, and expedites two-way communication to interpret and support the Church's mission through press office facilities, audio-visual materials, and a radio-television office.

Office of Stewardship

Responsible for stewardship training and education, planned giving, and the Venture in Mission program. Resources and assistance for dioceses and congregations available upon request.

Bibliography

Carr, Oscar C., Jr., ed., *Jesus, Dollars and Sense* (New York: The Seabury Press, 1976).
A workable theology for the stewardship of money.

Gray, William B. and Betty Gray, *The Episcopal Church Welcomes You* (New York: The Seabury Press, 1974).
A brief, up-to-date introduction to the history, worship, and mission of the Church.

Wallace, Bob N., *The General Convention of the Episcopal Church* (New York: The Seabury Press, 1976).
A concise history of the General Convention of the Episcopal Church.

Appendix II

Excerpts from Canon Law

TITLE I

CANON 6.
Of Business Methods in Church Affairs

Standard methods prescribed.

Sec. 1. In every Diocese, Parish, Mission, and Institution, connected with this Church, the following standard business methods shall be observed:

Deposit of funds.

(1). Trust and permanent funds and all securities of whatsoever kind shall be deposited with a Federal or State Bank, or a Diocesan Corporation, or with some other agency approved in writing by the Finance Committee or the Department of Finance of the Diocese, under either a deed of trust or an agency agreement, providing for at least two signatures on any order of withdrawal of such funds or securities.

Proviso.

But this paragraph shall not apply to funds and securities refused by the depositories named as being too small for acceptance. Such small funds and securities shall be under the care of the persons or corporations properly responsible for them.

Record of trust funds.

(2). Records shall be made and kept of all trust and permanent funds showing at least the following:

(a) Source and date.
(b) Terms governing the use of principal and income.

(c) To whom and how often reports of condition are to be made.

(d) How the funds are invested.

(3). Treasurers and custodians, other than banking institutions, shall be adequately bonded; except treasurers of funds that do not exceed five hundred dollars at any one time during the fiscal year.

Treasurers to be bonded.

(4). Books of account shall be so kept as to provide the basis for satisfactory accounting.

Books of account and audits.

(5). All accounts of the Diocese shall be audited annually by an independent Certified Public Accountant. All accounts of Parishes, Missions or other institutions shall be audited annually by an independent Certified Public Accountant, or independent Licensed Public Accountant, or such audit committee as shall be authorized by the Finance Committee, Department of Finance, or other appropriate diocesan authority.

All reports of such audits, including any memorandum issued by the auditors or audit committee regarding internal controls or other accounting matters, together with a summary of action taken or proposed to be taken to correct deficiencies or implement recommendations contained in any such memorandum, shall be filed with the Bishop or Ecclesiastical Authority not later than 30 days following the date of such report, and in no event, not later than September 1 of each year covering the financial reports of the previous calendar year.

(6). All buildings and their contents shall be kept adequately insured.

Adequate insurance.

(7). The Finance Committee or Department of Finance of the diocese may require copies of any or all accounts described in this Section to be filed with it and shall report annually to the Convention of the Diocese upon its administration of this Canon.

Report to Convention.

(8). The fiscal year shall begin January 1.

Fiscal year.

Sec. 2. The several Dioceses shall give effect to the foregoing standard business methods by the enactment of

Dioceses to enforce by Canon.

Canons appropriate thereto, which Canons shall invariably provide for a Finance Committee or a Department of Finance of the Diocese.

Encumbrance of property requires consent of Bishop and Standing Committee.

Sec. 3. No Vestry, Trustee, or other Body, authorized by Civil or Canon law to hold, manage, or administer real property for any Parish, Mission, Congregation, or Institution, shall encumber or alienate the same or any part thereof without the written consent of the Bishop and Standing Committee of the Diocese of which the Parish, Mission, Congregation, or Institution is a part, except under such regulations as may be prescribed by Canon of the Diocese.

All property held in trust.

Sec. 4. All real and personal property held by or for the benefit of any Parish, Mission or Congregation is held in trust for this Church and the Diocese thereof in which such Parish, Mission or Congregation is located. The existence of this trust, however, shall in no way limit the power and authority of the Parish, Mission or Congregation otherwise existing over such property so long as the particular Parish, Mission or Congregation remains a part of, and subject to this Church and its Constitution and Canons.

Confirmation of trust by Dioceses.

Sec. 5. The several Dioceses may, at their election, further confirm the trust declared under the foregoing Section 4 by appropriate action but no such action shall be necessary for the existence and validity of the trust.

TITLE III

CANON 23.
Of the Filling of Vacant Cures

Wardens to give notice to Bishop when Parish or Congregation becomes vacant.

Sec. 1. When a Parish or Congregation becomes vacant, the Churchwardens or other proper officers shall notify the fact to the Bishop. If the authorities of the Parish shall for thirty days have failed to make provision for the services, it shall be the duty of the Bishop to take such measures as he may deem expedient for the temporary maintenance of Divine services therein.

Sec. 2. No election of a Rector shall be had until the name

of the Member of the Clergy whom it is proposed to elect has been made known to the Bishop, if there be one, and sufficient time, not exceeding thirty days, has been given to him to communicate with the Vestry thereon, nor until such communication, if made within that period, has been considered by the Parish or Vestry at a meeting duly called and held for that purpose.

Bishop may communi-cate with Vestry.

Sec. 3. Written notice of the election, signed by the Churchwardens, shall be sent to the Ecclesiastical Authority of the Diocese. If the Ecclesiastical Authority be satisfied that the person so chosen is a duly qualified Minister, and that he has accepted the office, the notice shall be sent to the Secretary of the Convention, who shall record it. And such record shall be sufficient evidence of the relation between the Minister and the Parish.

Certificate to Ecclesi-astical Authority.

Sec. 4. A Minister is settled, for all purposes here or elsewhere mentioned in these Canons, who has been engaged permanently, or for any term not less than one year, by any Parish, according to the rules of the Diocese in which such Parish is located.

Ministers settled when engaged for at least one year.

Index